STONELIGHT

POEMS

STONELIGHT

Sarah McCartt-Jackson

Airlie Press
PORTLAND OREGON

2018

Airlie Press is supported by book sales, by contributions to the press
from its supporters, and by the work donated by
all the poet-editors of the press.

The Airlie Prize was made possible by a generous gift from

Dr. Carol Whitsel

P.O. BOX 82653
PORTLAND OR 97282
WWW.AIRLIEPRESS.ORG

EMAIL: EDITORS@AIRLIEPRESS.ORG

Cover and Book Design: Beth Ford, Glib Communications & Design

First Edition
ISBN: 978-0-9895799-7-1
Library of Congress Control Number: 2018937659

Printed in the United States of America

For my family and the hills I've wandered

and always, my Bryan

Vein of Stone

Children Born on the Wrong Side of the River

Flash Flood, Flash Fire

What You Hold

Kentucky Rose

This soil is a vein of stone the company calls *blue heron*
            to indicate its grade—
                        a bituminous grease in the pleats of eyelines
                    and thumbnail quick,
                                in the corners of Eli's mouth
        until everything tastes like the long coal throat of Mine 18,

soil which begins curled tight like an animal
            crouched beneath limed rock, like a mole
that burrows under the stonecrop and tickseed germ,
                slicking clay and loam. When the coal camp sleeps,
                                the dust skulks back
into the tipple rivets, into Eli's eyes brown as a bottle lip.
            Above him, miles of black ocean sag.

Five days and a riverside away from his wife Ora, Eli knows the rain
    by whether or not his ankles slap through coalwater,
                whether the sludgy drip of soil-seep oils his palm.

And when the earthhush of that shaft struggles to slip from the blue
        shale stitched above the carbon, the sound becomes the rasp
        of a carpenter bee's mandibles boring tunnels
                into the porchwood to remove its yellow poplar
            grain by grain, gram by spittled gram.

I

Vein of Stone

Homeplace

Here, an icicle melts into a pond of blue light,
opening mud, cake of earth shines

fishscale oilsheen, wrinkled rivershore

Ora nicks her fingernail on the broomhandle hickory
coaldust in the quilt seams, in the floor scars

Here, April sun distant-pale, April sun tart as an early apple

Here in the dusk cusp, deer know the storm-licked rims of drought

Eli the crunch between gravel and tire, Ora the peach

pulp sucked from the woody pit ridges

Here, the chilly spring raw as a bruise
struck by the earth beneath its perfect limb.

All Flesh Is Grass

Moonflowers opened their mouths
at night as they shied from daylight into pollen.

When Eli first slid into our bed,
      found me through the quilt,
cotton slipped between us like river, the flesh
of unripe apples sour on our tongues.

Goldenrod crept through a drought-shrunk August,
  stole rainwater with rootstocks.
Eli, I said, though I thought something else:
     cliff flood clay ash
I thought of a brush pile ready to burn.

Our love tunneled into stony silt loam,
a rhizome sapling difficult to uproot.

I dug my fingers into arid earth,
     spread my tendrils,
       scratching toward the farthest fence.

In the Hearth

Each room smells like dishsoap, rattles with the plates
in the metal sink, the fruit flies hovering
over the rag oily with vinegar and grease.

When he touches her, she slides away, her dreams
slipping beneath the cool side of the pillow
like a silverfish skidding between the plank floor knots.

She fingers the outline of the quilt squares
in the dark, each thread a stitched scrap,
each line a spider's leg tracing and retracing

the web it plaits and replaits every night.
A cricket scratches its legs together, a creak that breaks
the starched air between them. She thinks of his body

always like locking a door, like licking a thread
before needling the eye, like checking the length
of shadows in the yard, like picturing *lie, open, sail.*

His hand on her hip is an owl wing gliding,
a shadow through thick notes of locusts
as though there was a sound in it she was not hearing.

Finally, she turns to him to kiss, and she feels like gold light
pooling in the mouths of clematis vine, wraps herself around
that light like fence wire hewn to elm. Between her legs,

she feels the deep sleep found inside a walnut shell,
she feels as if her body contains some creatures hatching
in the deep trace of light, waiting for someone to love them.

Ora names her children
(before they are born)

unafraid of the shadow that glides up the mountain
approaching the nest. She names them the too-close sound
of a child's whisper inside her ear. She names them buds
on splintery sycamore limbs and the buds' curled leaves.
She names them after river clay and lightning shapes,
after songs she hears from the bucket dropped into the well.
She names them turnip and buckeye and leather and bird-feather hat
and tulip and the yellow color of rooms lit by flame.
She names them loneliness that can be rocked to sleep,
rooms haunted by dust that crawls in between the floorboards,
a thunderstorm of starlings crowding out the light. She names
the fingernails, the knees, pale eyelashes, tiny shoes,
caterpillar inching along the branch hung over the roof.
And when her upturned hands pile up with names, she pours
them onto every pinecone fallen empty of seed split through
the staves, every fur tuft stuck to bark, every quill hollow
poked through the pillow. She plants them until they return
stitched to the ridgeline bones. They tell her not to name them.

Broken Dishes

Along the hills
an echo drips into each ear
and stretches over the misery of trestles
rumoring to us of cities growling nearer to us, their smoke
chokes out chestnut and birchwood and river mussels,
their train horns bray too close to hear
beyond the sills.

Like mustard seeds
the words erupt from inside out,
splay over our yards and take root in our clotheslines,
reminding us of industries that live on soot and smelted coke.
We wake to hear this echo: raw chainsaw tines
ready to chew through us like drought
dismantles weeds.

Something in it
has unhinged our home like the jaw
of a rat snake sneaking to eat us from behind,
to wreck the shapes of our children's bodies in their beds, smashed broken
dishes, and then to slip back into the frostblind
April or the storm-licked maw of
ourselves boneknit.

The men go out.
We're watching death quit a body,
replaced by a black river of coal cars that heave
stone from one place to another to be burned, a pile of slag-soak
left behind. And a pile of umbragemen, burning,
tipplemen, breakermen on knee—
at once devout.

We send Eli
to the coal camp. He says not long,
he'll send money, only five days travel by shoe
leather, only one by horse and cart. Flood will tend the field, fit the yoke.
And Sweet Lily, for whom the world is budbreak-new,
will ask me, *Where do animals*
go to die?

Figure

We never saw a store over there
in our Pine Splint holler but here the company
nailed together whitewash and planks
a pantry a commissary where with metal-
disc and cardboard scrip stamped
with the company name we paid their prices

Their blue denim shirt cost a dollar
where in Pineville it's 47 cents
A dollar and ought for overalls
a man could get in Pineville at 64¢
Company tools at three-fifty
sold in Pineville at one buck eight

I am my brass tag I am number 42
I am the number 42 car I haul to the weighman
who figures less than the stone I cut
and dug with a number nine shovel
for a hundred two-inch holes in the coalface

And I pay for the dynamite   a piece of paper
and 30¢ for powder to shoot the coal
and lamp carbide to burn a nickel
a week and room rent and doctor bill
and union borrow fund and coal and sledge
and wedge and mule feed and pick and auger and
tool sharpen fee and meat and lard and
flour and salt and shoes and shoes
and shoes. All the rest they say is mine.

My Dearest Eli,

I hold the coal so close to my eye, I only see the root-dark
of its past. Tell me how this *blue heron* was a loamy lagoon. Tell me
that where your pick and wedge displaced coal, a floodplain once splayed
along a river lacing channels of shells. Tell me the glassy surface
of slickensides reflects a siltstone lake, tell me the spark of mica in the stackrock
reminds you of barbed-wire stars.

Leave out the scars of split slate, the spalling
limestone, its horseback-shaped slabs that crush men. I want to think of the ridgeland
as a hand pushing on the watery edges of the spur's old swamp. Leave out
how Pine Splint is a body with shaly-walled arteries and clay skin
and each of you a little bit of blood slaking roughness from the core. Leave out
how the hilltop spills down into the valley, releases the body's weight settling the belly.
How the fractures unfasten. How the ribs collapse inward. The fissured rock
leaving a new fossil rolled in a kettlebottom. The cast iron an ancient tree trunk.
Where you see just one, there blooms a dark forest of veins.

your Ora

Gulch

She could not sleep. There
when evening mushroomed
through the porchwood, the spiderlegs
of light spread out across the hollow,
      poplar cups clutching each stray webstrand,

  she could not sleep
without thinking of the pine barn leaning
toward the valley, of the creekbed
filling with iron, lime, and mouse bones.
      And Eli, gone to the camp just one week.

That week roils forward heavy with storm,
each day whipped into a frothy pool of half-night:

  she hears the air chewing
through her sleep creaky with rocking
back and forth, forth and back, sees the green
      eyeshine of an owl blink from the birch.

  If it flies left of the house: withered crops, spoiled eggs.
If it flies right: healthy children, no cornmold, Eli in November.
And should she fly directly over: a loss, a cave thick with water,
      a slab of bedrock sunk beneath a lake.

  Her wingtips drag like rain over the roof edge
touching both eaves at once, and Ora knows
the shade as a sadness gloaming inside her
      home—a family of quail scuttling into the thicket.

Harvest Blues

Rise at 5 before the sun. Put on your clothes. Eat breakfast. Walk three miles to the mine. Arrive. Buy your dynamite, your sharpened coal pick and boring auger, your dinner pail with half a gallon of water. Think of ham salad and meatloaf and the sweet taste of wellwater. Collect your brass tag that reminds you who you are. Walk three miles to your workface. Arrive. Remove your outer coat and shirt. Work in your undershirt. Bang the flat end of a stick on the roof to examine stability. Listen for vibrations in your feet and hands. If you feel it swell with sound, stay. Think of your daughter, sweet humming, picking wild onions. Put a support under the roof to secure it. It is secure. Now drill a hole with your auger into the coalface. Drill more holes. Roll a newspaper sheet into a tube shape and crimp the end. Pour in black powder. Think of your son's first turkey shoot and his face when you gave him the rifle. Crimp the edge closed. Pierce your cartridge with a needle. Shove it in the drilled hole. Tamp it. Thrust in a handful of fine coal dust collected from the coal ribs. Ram it back. Repeat until you fill the hole. Withdraw the needle. Think of your wife's feet slipped into a cool creek, her homespun blouse you could see through at an angle just so in the dusk. Place the blasting cap on. Fire the fuse. A chunk of coal the size of an egg breaks loose. Pick it up. Load it into your mine car. Put your brass tag on the nail in car. Repeat repeat repeat repeat repeat repeat repeat repeat until full. Push your car three miles to the tipple. Blink in the daylight. Repeat.

Double Wedding Ring

The water surges and raises the silt,
which lines the valley bellies with yellow slurry.

As mud eddies inside the hearth
and coagulates the fireplace ashes,

Ora remembers her own wedding
like sweeping a broom through bloodroot,

their marriage the splink
of rust-warm rain on a tin roof,

his touch like goldenrod pollen
in the small space between her legs.

Her *yes* was the bell of jonquil cones,
his voice a bucket rattling with gravel.

Board and Batten

1. Clearing

All the trees were already gone
burning in their hillside stumps,
piles of ashes, brittle doe eyes
black and sunken, looking into the earth
instead of starward

then come a tide to carry them off
rush their trunks downriver
to be dried and planed, board and batten
that make up our camp buildings
row after straight-edged row

2. Blasting

We tamp down the dynamite, split the rock
        strata, splinter each slate slice, shattered plates
            of frozen mud, shocked out of crags,
        gray-cold slivers stuck one by one

into our hearts, tucked into the farthest corners
        and rows of our paychecks,
            licked envelope torn seal

She swears our wild children have followed me here
        that they thrust their fists out of the rockcuts
            clutch our lamplight, drape it on the walls, gather light
            like faces gathering

3. *Digging*

Where have all the breakermen gone
who worked with me on the dragline
They shed their skin, flake by flake
their rust-colored shadows grow tall
22 stories high taller than the tipple
carrying buckets of slate and rock
lungs filled with each other's coughs,
their shovels nudge each granite pit
rake through the memory of plowed fields
strain to smell the taste of a riverbottom field
slightly copper, slightly salt

4. *Dumping*

overburdened mules, endless leather tackle,

                                     bridled to a cart
how each cart dumped into a railcar
forms a dustcloud that feeds on ascending sun warmth
and looms over the tipple, straight up

how each man bends and turns away, the creature at his back
rumbles, the mine mouth at his face reaches out its gritty fingertips
taps silently on each lamp, intimidates the flame

5. *Processing*

Where have all the tipplemen gone
who worked with me in the cold coalwater
harp-eyed boys on the loading booms
who measure their worth in slate and bone:
nut and slack: the size of your fingers making an o
egg: the size of your wife's hollowed palm
and block: the size of your two fists
cuffed against my two fists, or a brick

We wash ourselves of the excess day
Watch water pour from the bucket clean
Watch sludge clay slurry away foul

6. *Reclamation*

We keep near the tipple a mountain
of low-grade coal dumped and heaped
shouldered against exposure
As the mountain grows, something deep within
sparks a spontaneous fire which breaks
out, spreads, and burns inexorably

And each night the fire dies. And each day it rises again.

Salt of the Earth

I like my job
not the mine
I like how
the carbide lamp
spoils light
on the coal face
that goes down
down, down

Cool smell
of wet clay
grit of sand
stone under
my boot going
down, down
down

I like to be
a breath
in the rustle
of the mine's
cave and feel
the give
beneath
my wedge
hear the chunks
rattle down,
down, down

The cough
I carry
in my lung the
thin way I
take my air
I don't mind
much when I'm down
down, down

because each room
collects
the dust of where
I've been
each column
silts my lips
my cough

slips out
on all fours
and crawls down
down, down

But to watch
a place you love
get gone

To be the man
who does it.

Dearest Eli,

        I don't want a new house or painted walls or to live near where I can hear the sirens wake us. I don't want coins or gold or silver or paper dollars or canned food. I don't want a new stove or an electric bulb. I don't want a box that stores ice, a new neighbor that doesn't sing because she can't hear over the trainhorn wailing. I don't want you gone, deep down. I don't want your picked waves that lick the coal shores, your scraped away ancient shoals, your deliberate tipple, rock toppled hills. I don't want your ring roped on my hip.

        Give me the rope that you tied around my finger, wild grapevine warped into a loop. Give me your face, your hands cupping my breasts, your shoes filled with your mud and feet. Give us your crooked back aching, your owl-lidded eyes, your breath in our ears, our handplanes, our spindles, our hums, our ladles, and we will
   give you back
your money, your ring, your footprints in the corn, your tart apples picked from your tree that make your mouth and tongue water.

your Ora

Moonroot

The breaker boys say for me
to chew the moonroot they say
it works they say the calamus root
sticks to you like a lung
to a rib. They say it prevents it
with spit and to pray to a tea of
chimney soot, a long dark song
in each cough just out of reach.

II

Children Born on
the Wrong Side
of the River

She dreams of muddy water

of her children watching her trace the oak knot floor, of wind that stirs inside the chimney, of seven kinds of rain, of the roots that will not stop accumulating in her, of old coyotes that do not chase prey, of pine needle rugs hooked by a good fire, of her children as linen, of the empty mailbag rumpled on a chairback, of fields sown in an old moon, of unlit homes housing unlit rooms.

Our father,

I heard you in the well your watery voice dripped
from the mossy edges of limestone I called you by your name and
not by father or daddy or pop because we are grown now in the well
Flood dropped your watch I heard the metal scrape the walls and
plunk into the soil-tasting water imagined what the gears felt like as
they stopped their ticking like the sound of picks underground each
of our steps a thunder to you beneath us each one of us with one ear
pressed to the field we lie in the corn beds looking down the rows and
at each other we imagine we hear you in the boneset inching its way
up the stalks the smell of earth in our water the taste of copper on our
plow I know you're down the well I hear you

love Lily

Migration

The starlings began to fall from our birch trees
like seeds, black bodies thudded, rolled
off our roofs into downspouts and gutters.
Shingles scraped the feathers. Bird bones snapped
like dry cornhusks inside their soft throats.

But the starlings kept coming, littering our bark
peeled away like ash, torturing the timber
on our plot, giant flocks rattling on branches
until we buried the last ones, our yard
pocked with clay mud that smelled like snakes.

Then: a voice came through swollen grains
of goldenrod pollen, stuck to every anther,
sloped over milkweed pods opened and spilled,
struck river mussel flesh in their shells,
enough to fill an empty turtle shell, a silo, a rusty-lidded jar.

The Buck Moon grew its way out of sycamore,
deer antlers spread velvet light on our faces, coyotes
clawed and nosed the mounds, threw the bird bodies
up into the air, catching them in teeth ravenous
and swallowing whole. Even dirt in which the starlings lay.
Even the spaces between their bones.

Weather (Lily)

I saw the storm coming in our cows the way they will lie
down in fields and the birds fly low overhead the locusts
sang like roosters crowing momma dropped the beans
on the floor picked up each one one by one *pting pting*
back in the pot back over the smokeline from the cookstove
gray fingerspreading pine splint was cloudshrouded so I knew
we had six hours at best the chickens hovered near
open doorways Flood kicked a hen on his way inside a rusty hinge
announcing him brought momma your leathers leaves turned
underside showed their white bellies I didn't tell her but
   a black widow
began her web too early in autumn set her legs into the sticky silk
momma couldn't know how an owl sounds more like crying
people than birds or how chimney smoke rises into the sky
    but seems to settle
down around our home until the spring sun turns back and
    the valley burns

Flux

When the milkcow hadn't spared a drop even for the calving when its udder shriveled like a rotting pawpaw Ora carried sweet Lily white as an onion bulb for five days to that company doctor in his tie and all the miners paying $2 for medical whether sick or well this being taken off the salary and that doctor in his tie gave Ora the pills to crush up and put in sweet Lily's water in sweet Lily's throat, so, with sweet Lily on her hip Ora walked five days home hauled the bucket from the creek to her house three times a day sweet Lily's head hanging back limp as a shot opossum each day getting sicker than the day before so when the doctor in his tie rode by Eli on his horse Eli said *Doctor look at my child* and the doctor went to licking his thumb and wetting his scuffed boot and saying *She's alright* and sweet Lily each day shrinking down more behind her eyelids until on that Sunday sweet Lily's funeral uncoiled from the church bells like a sawbriar vine.

Wild Onions

Fireflies, tiny yellow heartbeats
outside Ora's window, tap the edges

of the panes, their glassed faces shine
in the onion-bulbed lantern:

Twelve children and so many gone
but who would not leave her:

Lily was flame-wing smoke,
the shuffle of feet. Prairie was sigh
of the green beans' opened lid. Alva was
bloodroot that blooms for one day
on a hillside ripe with Homer who was
liverwort burst from bouldersprings.
Eldred, second, had no middle name.
Opal was the hush of snow piled
on a limb. Ola B the wind that shook it.
Elmer was rivershore mud song
mushing up between your toes. And Ruby
was fistfuls of clover ripe to eat. Sharon was
eldest, who lived long and longer
than the rest. Hobie the horse
who chewed a hole through barnwood.

Company

The only road there snakes through Horse Lick Creek
to their cedar-and-sycamore plank walls, where some
of her children sit at a hand-hewn table of knotty pine,

and others—who appear from the porch, leafshade,
rockhill fieldrows—peek into the windows, their faces
gather like light, their bodies smell like mud and rain.

Eli uses a whittled stick to light his tobacco, each minute
a black smudge slithering up the burnt stick-tip. His fingertips,
sooty and yellow-nailed. Winter hisses through the chimney
throat like frozen pond water cracking. He says he will be gone again
once he buries sweet Lily, once she unrolls her song in the fiddlehead fern.

And through the wake's hours: Ora cries into her left hand,
Eli stirs a spoon against the sides of his glass, tinkling
through milk and whiskey, stitching smoke to his skin,
her bones like empty soupcans. The children stare
at the folded hands in their laps. Ora shakes like a hill collapsing.

Honeycomb

Eli cut lumber out of his ceiling,
took to hammer and saw,
slipped out the nails one by one, pocketed
them in his overalls

one by one. Each bowed board crashed
to their floor, damp with mold
and rot and bare seasons sweet Lily
will never see no more.

Eli stacked his pine boards one by one
on the slatted porch rail wall,
made sweet Lily's coffin from their home
and he spackled the knots

so she would not look through the wood,
would not watch him shovel
bottomland soil into a hole as deep
as bedrock level.

And now Eli has a ceiling high
that peeks through holes in the roof,
swollen-dark nighttime eyes
and Eli wonders who

will listen for his pick ticking
when he returns to shore,
the sound of water under water,
sweet Lily will never see no more.

Grieving

You think you are fine, will always be fine. You braid your hair. You think about not washing the dishes. You buy a box of milk, sign and mail the burial plot papers, peel paint from the dining room chair, or address letters to your husband at the coal camp. Chickens peck at grit in the yard but there's not enough cornbread to scrape from the skillet, so you prepare a boiling pot to pluck and slaughter the scrawniest bird. You splinter the unfinished chair on the porch steps. When your face floats in the scummy pond or in your hand-mirror in the woodburning light or over the dark pupils of your other daughters, you beg to be let go, burn a hymn into the air until your voice blisters each oak knot in your plank walls. You pull the quilts closer, feel winter creep over your toes. You feel bloodless but do not sleep, your night wide and heavy with the mountain. You listen to your children breathing through the shale. You whisper, *Shhhh, shhhh.*

Interlude

These moments happen. Suddenly—
$$\text{a stitch drops off}$$
  the needle, bares cold the metal.
Those clacking sounds. Cease.

And when you look through
  yourself in the mirror, the silver
sheet is only an ugly face. A thin lip.
$$\text{A pleat creased,}$$

starched into another pant leg.

There is no lace
  in the hinge of your knee.
  But there is *yes*
flat as planed pine, *yes* graver
      than a diamond,

Yes in a cattail grating
on the sleeve of a reed.

Your womb blooming again.

Jacob's Ladder

They say children born on the wrong side
of the river grow wild as fleabane
  and do not return until Spring,
   their veins all grass stems and cricket legs,

and that wild scuttles straight from their eyes
   over the creekbed and slips over the birdfoot violet
                  into the sandstone,

       A mother cannot look at them directly—
      their pupils might crumble like dry mud under a thumb.

     But Ora could not get to the other bank
        for the flood washing the river's cobble
           and the mussels loose from their shells
     and her husband gone back to the coal camp.

So her baby's hands uncurled as bluet and phlox,
     her heart a hard walnut, shriveled and shut,
   her bloody mouth a kiss on her mother's thigh.

Dear father,

Our mother has done something strange in your absence.
I'm not convinced you will ever come home. Are you there? How is the mine?
Are you a breaker man? Or are you on the coal face? Mother has done
  something.
You should know. I was looking for the axe so I could ready some wood.
But I couldn't find it. I asked her, *Where is the axe?* She said she didn't know.
I know she knows. So I looked for it. And I asked sweet Lily. And I asked
all the others out there. And I don't know how to explain this, but the others
  told me
where to look. So I looked under mother's bed. And the axe was there. Sunk
in a floor plank like it was just waiting to sleep there and be ruined by moss.
I asked her why it was there. She grabbed her baby belly. She ran to the river.
When she came back, she was naked. But I found her nightgown, bloodied by
  the water.
I hope you will come home soon. Or please send a nickel.

Your son, Flood

Dear Eli,

        I have heard we purchased a dark and bloody ground
here where the mouth of a bass is a wound, an open and black bruise
on our skin, an axe sunk in mud, a hunger hung frayed from the tulip
poplar branch, but we cannot remove ourselves from this
field bottom where palisades cut river in limestone fossil-laced
with rib and spine something glistens on the water
like the blinking eyeshine of barn owls, feathers gray
as sheets of shale, brown as limp tobacco veins.

Here where once a coal camp lay rail and tie miles, where traincars
sucked trees and stone out like bellow sacs, the land tilled turned
split raked burned, the fields never left fallow so that the river bleeds
rust-colored slag rather than blue. In the grass that reclaims the crumbling
tipple, our now-dead clatter with steel children shoveling
more coal more coal, eyes blink out beneath their sooty faces.

Ora

Homecoming

Born on the river's wrong side,
we are the March weather that spits wind
  in the eaves of your house, the recluse spider
        hidden in your rolled up kitchen towel. We are the wobble
  in the loops of your handwriting, the trembling shadow
  you cannot shake from the creases in your stationery.

We are the shifting field in your chest, the rust in your wellwater.
That splintering crack of gunshot during an otherwise silent migration.

        You know we are
  the presence that scatters harvesting birds
        from your birch tree branches. You know
  we are the bonewhite spaces of bark and trunk left behind.

And when the doctor exposes the knob
  in your lung, when your ruined womb releases,
when your husband says he can no longer try
to be away from you, when the fires shake your house

and lick your children's hairbows

and eat their tiny shoes, we crawl into your stomach

and open it so wide

you think the air might be dampening, think a bat might be hanging

like a tongue in the cave of your heart.

But because every day you pass through the same spaces

where we have been, you shudder less: Because when we

leave a room,

you enter the closing hole of sifting particles

and make your heart larger:

We are also the sweetness of an overripe apple straining to the edges

of its peel,

the hard seeds between your teeth, the white flash

of juice running down your chin. We are the stain

and the color, the flesh and the still life, the shadow beneath

a wooden bowl

and the light gathered on its rim.

Windmill

Where it all sparkled, green-river-filled birds' nests, blue eggs cradling tiny beating hearts, flowers made in glass, pressed carnelian and cut shaved opal, the pearlsmooth lip of a river mussel shell. The living in us was butterflies, was crickets, was flown and leaped, knew each fern spore, each sassafras root, teaberry leaf waxy and wet in our cheeks. If we could tell of the unending sentence of love that vines out of us, clings to sunlight, a yellow trout lily that blooms on an outcrop in a fistful of sandy soil, roots sunk through each crack, its question mark stem answered by water-trickled petals that drain into a rockhole. If we could tell how when we lie asleep eyes and hands drinking the dark, how we refill those pools each morning with salt-white light that reaches into our pockets, floods us with wildness waiting.

Weathervane

When the cow dies, Ora touches her five children,
   their mouths wide as magnolia blooms, holes
for which there were never enough rabbits to shoot and skin,
   or river mussels from the sycamore shoals.
The hush becomes the weather rushing through that holler,
            their empty stomachs the last leaves rimed with frost
becomes what the weather rushing through that holler tells her:
            Find a hickory tree scabbed over with moss

            among timber fires in their stumps that smolder on the hillside
            like the burning oil of many lamps.
            Even a foaming wild dog cannot drink the water it finds
                        in a winter dark as the blue flame of black damp.

My Dearest Eli,

                    The spring peepers cling to the trees, our rooms
the shape of chirping, and I'm starting to believe I can hear the shadow
of an owl's open wings swooping over the soft-rotten leaves,
an appleseed shoot pushing from a mushy core. Tonight's sunset
ashened in the cow's lowing as she lay down to pasture
her bones. Night swells mud-thick as the river floods
our steep gap. I am thinking of you in the burrows of rockspur
and the lattice-light tearing beneath the riverstone. Your name slowly turns

our soil over the plow's tongue, the space between a rattled walnut, its woody shell.
I feel your breath in the green-cut meat of the season's saplings, but do you hear me
as your body rises through the poplar sap? See how the wing-shade shudders
through my heart when I remember you here, when I cup your face, plant it
in every magnolia bud. And I think each day the night settles back in the hollows
because the dark has nowhere else to go.

your sassafras, your Ora

Dear Father
                    I found you today I thought
you were in the well but now I know you are not
I heard you in the limestone trying to come
out trying to get your body out of the place
you placed it I touched the dipped part
of the cliff where you fell asleep and your body
piece by piece went into the stone I heard
you in there like gravel pops under tires
trying to find a crack I will tell momma how
you lay down one day by this stream
against the cliff face and how each day the rock
opened a hole further and further until you became
part of the rock and how you live there now
she will be glad to know you were swallowed whole

                                        love Lily

flash flood,

flash fire

Cloudburst

Sudden downpour:
        tributaries and brooks swell, gush over
        streambeds and shoals, sink and tumble through
            eddies surged to chutes, steal houses, swim them
        into trees, trees stick in trees, rain pounds metal
        roofs, plank porches, cornfields, apple orchards
shredded thread by blossom threaded with rain

water spills down the hillsides in sheets
        seven inches deep in the shallowest places
        laid-by logs rainswept away
            river-flattened frame houses, riverstone foundations
        reclaimed planks whirl out into the beds
        of surging rivers where corn stood sprouting, rising
stalk by stalk the afternoon before and all

the bridges broken in damp onslaught
        of living rooms filling with mud hollows sagging
        like cornshuck beds beneath water weight
            and wrack and unemployed men stand on rooftops
        rub their chins, shake their heads, watching
        mountains of slate crash into streams, makeshift dams
struggle against water, shrug, landslide away,

rage against bent rails, split ties, torrent spewed and plunging
our unclean bodies, rushed and wrinkle-ripened come dawn.

Black Damp

When collected on the workfaces of beams and spokes and spars and elsewhere in the mines. And when conditions are aright can explode with a power of dynamite shot from the face, a dry place saturates air with millions of dancing particles of dust. When a wirespark or when lampflame ignites it, how it surges—roars—how a cough sounds inside a lung. And when dust-filled air snores on the coal ribs and timbers. When the explosion races down headings, entryways and coal rooms until the fuel lays by, lies down, sleeps, exhausted in its smoke-made blanket. Chainlike. Linked in seconds or minutes as the fire tumbles like a river from one to another. When the fiery tornado reaches its finger out and strokes each stubbled miner's chin, curls inside empty pockets, fills each dark hole. When a yellow tongue flicks out of the driftmouth without a sound: a siren.

Fractureslip

Imagine the flood beginning with children
how they made the river at the beginning of time:
they went in separate directions at night,
walked a mile over the surface and put down
a stone, then another mile: a stone, another mile:
a stone. Thusly they weaved a stream, riven
and bearing each creature, two by two, on boats
made of seed pods, fallen leaves, timbered
logs snagged in a high limb.

                                 The water separates itself
as a bird separates from its voice when flying,
sheds its *birdie birdie birdie* like lice in its wings
of feathered sky. A flood of beetles that ate your
turkey feathers, nothing left but featherspines.
A flood of glozed coal that waits beneath sycamore bark
ready to curl and peel away, whittled piles lost
in floods of clover, floods of locust drones in the storm-wrack
and scouring rush, floods of animal hearts racing
for higher ground, floods of frogs plunked into mud
over the storm-gored gorge.

Slickensides

Suddenly pale flame
          the sound of tamping
the sound of owl talons
click click clicking
in walnut trees, the sound of
lampflame shadows bumping
against the ceiling like mothwings
gone into the root-laced dark,
slipped into the cracks
the shape of lightning.

The ground shook
like a horse's flank,
rippled with muscle
and stamped
the caked mud from
its cracked horseshoes.

The sound of each
minecar of coal rattled into the tipple.
It was like the naked stone
began to wander in the puddles
around their feet, frayed.

The sound of each sooty figure
riding the mantrip on his back,
each gray face slipped one by one
out of the mine mouth.

Looks like cloud-shadows
passing over the hollow.
Looks like death leaving
a body of rain-soaked woodplanks.

Hear the hooves come thundering home.
Hear darkness gathering darkness in a fist.

Slake

Everywhere we are is a shoreline, an ancient ocean
that looms in rock filled with animals ready to rise
again and swallow each of us, except the ones that cannot be
swallowed. So Ora stood at her yard's edge, the edge of her coast
shrieking like a screech owl when it happened—
This animal clawed down into her lungs, pressed itself
against her heart, and cleaved itself to her limbs, stem
by stem. A drought that crimped the lonely in her veins.

Hunger

What was there left
to do? He felt the stackrock
roofslick and shaly.
Saw mica sparkle
in the clay. It heaved
bottom up, cracked
like a spine, coal ribs
limed in dust.
Small specks of flame.
What was there left
to do? He ate the crumbs
from his dinner pail
looked into the dark,
turned into a bear.

Kettlebottom

The house
has been
the scarred round space
of a cut oak limb.

A silence
roars
between rafters,
roosts
in the sink.

The outside
slinks in
like a dog
that has eaten
the roast.

She feeds it
until
it grows old
until it has fallen
into
its eyes.

Rooting

At first, he thought the light moved
like a coyote rent from its pack.
But that is how the light sounded.

Now, the light moves like a bear,
black and shining fur, lumbers farther
around each corner into the shiftlight,
trudges its weight around

the bend, into the woods
a trail of stone tongues flickers,
snuffed out and dredged.

He burdens the trail, hobbles
like a bear's sagged belly. Becomes it.

Suddenly, it was like the stone
was where it was supposed to be.
Dragged him to where he was
supposed to be.
                    He lies down
his back against the stackrock.

His sleep heavy with the mountain.

And every so often he wakens, stretches
his hands out against dark, notices
a dip forming in the rock. And every night he slips

his curved body back into the deepening
shallow, sleeps in the groove he makes
of his body. Each night he gives to the sleepload
that fractures and spreads its paws, roars within
him, within them both, them all, all of us.

Thirst

She ate salt. Salt licks. Salted ham. Salty dirt beneath the hams.
She didn't drink water for three days. Four days. Her lips cracked.
She salted them. She had a stream that was hers. She knew it was hers.
She didn't look at it except from the corner of her eye. Afraid it would leave
if it knew it was hers. Then she walked to it. Stood with her mouth open
before the water. Let the sound of riverrock fill her mouth. She stood for hours,
open, tongue-foamed. Until the animal got thirsty, bucked from her body
like young buds shoot through snow-gripped roots to light.

Spall

It was like nothing
was happening at all
like all the veins
in all the leaves stopped
drinking water or sunlight
like all the tree stumps
stopped rotting, stopped
taking seed into their broken torsos.
It was like seeing a body
and knowing it would never wake.
It was like seeing a body and thinking
it might wake. It was like waking
a body with the silence
of another body. It was like nothing
on earth mattered: a skink
sun-basked and bathed
crumpled paper on the ground
and it was like no one knew me
and no one got to know me
and no one should
know me but everyone should know
me. It was like collapsing and
melting and hugging and not
hugging. Like pressing your bare
chest to a cold stone that fit the shape
of your body and then hating
the stone but not being able
to let go of it. It was like wanting
wanting to drink more milk,
wanting to eat potatoes
with cheese, wanting to know
your favorite color, your favorite song
what it sounds like when you sing
your voice when you called me
cliff flood ash clay.

Compass

When springtide ends, Ora cuts her arm off
to count the rings—two for each season. None

for summer. The glacier-melt begins to rise from her

chest light as bodyshells of insect-molt:
something that tiptoes between light and dark.

Chain and Square

He likes to think he farms stone.
Every coalroom is a planted row.
Black shades of crop fall
to his sickle his blade,
his auger uproots.
He spreads his fingers
out on the roof
like how he might
test a thirsty sky
to feel the vibrations:
how the earth breathes
how it doesn't
how it tries to cough
him out of its throat.

What Ora Heard
(after the Mine 18 siren)

She heard the long yawn of a cat, and saw its mouth
like a sky full of high clouds milk-white and cold-stung.
Cloudburst emptying rain on the field, field mice
rushing for unflooded furrows. His voice the sound
of the last leaves falling, wet and frost-rimed. Every night
broke open like a chrysalis, and a thousand insects scrabbled out.
It was the sound of teeth marks on bone and a ripe coal
burning blue then red then—

she heard and hated a train horn wedged in her chest,
felt a trembling black river of coal stumble at the tipple
of his lips, raw sound that was his voice
but not his words, just groans scraping his body
on their way out, just moans scratching through his hands
that quivered and shook out the sound stuck in him.

She heard a hawk, its call needled through her ear, its hoarse
kee-eeeee-arr shone like a white thread in the brown branchlight.
And somewhere on a limb, high in a poplar, she saw him,
naked and plumed, calling: mirrored lake
sound, pierced and frightened—just a jaybird
stuck in its nest, limb-swayed and empty.

Foxfire

The light approaches like a black horse and muddy water,
like crossing over a river, like being lost in a cave when a light
calls as an echo: *Come near, come near, come near.*

Gathering light in his pupils he sees
how light ripples toward you, blue holes on slag,
minewater drip on his thirsty tongue. Waterlight

ashes into coaldust he builds a fire of. He almost licks the lips
of the overhang, the puddled slosh beneath his boots, a blue-
black eye that says drink me or die, drink me or die. This is it:

the light of a white dog after dark that stops to look at him,
says the name of a dead person that erupts as flame,
whose blue core turns into a narrow woodland trail,

a trail that follows between the base of dead trees, each groan
a hollow bone creak in his legs, where lightning has struck by
the sloped mudshale and three footprints of a rabbit lost.

A furry light which hops like a dream but when he reaches
for it, dragging each leg, licking his teeth—That is how the light moves away.

IV

What You Hold

Log Cabin

And somewhere smoke unrolls like a pine needle, unspooling
    from a red oak root clutching unhatched larvae,
    from the powder of the failed chimney chinking,
    from the fallen petals of cinquefoil and cross-vine,

a smoke that repeats the story:

    Once there was a heron that spread her wings
to the edge of Kentucky where she dragged her feathertips
along fence planks and doorway eaves, on every toe
    and dirt-wrinkled sole of each foot on each white ash floor.

    When the earth opened, she crawled into the hole of its mouth
    and flew away with seventeen men on each wing
and left a rock that sank on their tongues,
    their hands in the limestone soil heavy as wellwater,
    their voices grain between two millstones.

Their home a crow's nest of barbed wire.

Dear Eli, appleseed,

                                 This is what you miss:
collarbone ridgetop knobs,
back pond scooped and skin-dipped,
sweat pooled between the shoulderblades
                                   of feather-rag fog.

You always forget a hawk until you see it
sliding on the edges of air and sinking
into crisp-leafed hillsides that breathe:

their ribcaged timber rises like breadloaf, ferns exhaling
each cool night, each sucked-in gasp of day,
the mist flooding your lungs

You like the feel of each yeasty plume
curling into the holy warmth
you swallow, the way it feels
like it's swallowing you
                        your Ora

Laying Ghosts

They say drive four iron nails into the corners of the grave before a green sky can turn them. Drive the ghost into the body of a crow, into a sheepfold, into a catskin. Walk round the last place you saw them nine times. Remove the door. Hang it backwards. Bury a church bell in one pond. The clapper in another. Don't bring a digging tool into the house. Or you will dig a grave before the year is out. Don't let the tool rest against a wall inside. Everyone left will fall ill. Feed the ghosts potato soup. Slip wild mustard under each pillow. Sink an axe in the floorboard beneath your bed to prevent another dead child. Black snake root. Cowslip. Poultice of nettles, tobacco juice, and ragweed. Rub it on your cheeks, your palms, the tops of your feet. Don't sing. Don't drink black walnut. Don't look in a mirror after dark. Or do. Bless their bodies with apple blossoms. Fix their faces—portraitless nails in your mind. Dead children who return only want to stop their parents weeping. Dead husbands want to help knit socks, piece quilts. Open up your hope chest. Unfold the folded quilts. Count the new seams, the new tying on.

Dearest Eli,

       Remember that corn-spoiled rooster, his thornspurs.
Remember how you loved to hear that crowing. And the night
you died that rooster crowed all night long. He did not
stop. All night long. Remember how you sat on the edge of our yard
crowing. You crowed about how there is a rooster in each of us strutting
on the graves we carry until we can lay them down on hillsides
like crooked teeth. It enters us before we are born and hides as arms
in our sleeves, tiny hairs on our ankles. Listen to me now. I see now

how sleep is the skin of your last harvest, your chest a shifting field.
Each corn stump a forest of bird legs stretching beneath the ground
into that root-laced dark. Each of us carries the grave, the field, the flame
of a rooster crowing on walnut logs in the rafter brace. When you hold
the note of a rooster in your throat, what you hold is no longer a bird.
It is the night we create in the clutch of our hands, crouched in our feathers.

Supper

When the moon is in the heart, she weeds.
When the new moon brings oak leaves young to bud,
she plants corn and with each row a stone.

She does not plant when the moon is in the heart or head.

She feeds them cucumbers when the moon is in the arms,
lettuce and cabbage on the old moon in April.
She feeds them wild berries after September,

dried apple cores and pears picked on a new moon in July.

She feeds them pinecones and peaches when the moon
is in the limbs, sassafras bark and honeysuckle,
an iron nail sunk in the breadloaf in May.

She walks down the porch steps, at midnight, she stoops.

Rubs her hands in the first snow, sets down each plate
in the yard. Wipes snow-wet on the doorsill,
and when the moon is in the bones, she feeds them

beets and rotting potatoes so they never come home.

Dear Sir,

        Momma asked us to write you, but I know better.
I know what has happened. I know how the plow
ends up in my hands. I know how a mother dyes
her cloth with red root and pine tar. I gathered
the walnut hulls myself. I chopped the wood for her
stove. I know how the smoothed ruts of the axe handle
splinter between your thumb and palm. I know the flint
and gun lock and powder and blade. And I know how they move
from your bedside to mine, like this:
simmering for a long time over a very intense heat
mix tobacco juice, hoary nettles, and ragweed into paste.
I pulled a poker from our fireplace and stuck it through my hand.

Flood

Burying

Do not look back after you leave the cemetery
  wild with Dead Man's Bells
          (or they will follow you, step each foot inside
          your print, their tiny toes inside your sole).
At the clearing edge, pick up a stone, carry it
in your right hand until you have passed—

          there where the day before a blackbird rested
          on your windowsill coaxed into your home, hopped
          onto the floor, thrust its head into the woodbeams,
          snagged a maggot from the wall and flew out the hole.
          Its wings sounded like clothes flapping on the line.

—carry it with you until you have passed the boundaries
of the yard, a stone in your hand, a caw in your throat
until the edges of wood erupt into straight-strung poplars.
Then set it down without looking back.

Dear Eli,

If I wish it deep as wellwater will you show me a sign? Will you
call me in the arch of my feet when they step on riverstone? Will you
gurgle through the mud beneath the quartz cobble, lick between
my toes? Will you edge the sandstone cliff be the ledge-tongue
that doesn't crumble when I climb? Will you river your song hard
as iron seams into these limestone gullies? Will you—will you—will you—

That poplar sapling pulled down by a swinging girl, bouncing over the river-
lip muddy with poison ivy and bank-cut steps, that sapling snapped
straight in me as a spine   pine oak maple sunray like a marble vein flattened
into a buffalo trace forked stream lapping the log swells and frog throat tug

You said Kentucky's valleys were warm as a womb, summers wet as hymns
cliffs hung like rough-shed snakeskin   you said the sunlight winging
from each leaf-verge trembled in the valley of your heart. But the mountain
ridgestone curls upwards   a fingerbone hooked   sickled smile

Attic Windows

We are the holly leaf rattle pattern.
>   The placental edges. We eat
>   the hard berries. The flood that bore us. Hauled us all
>   away when there come a tide.

We are bloodroot caul. We bleed. We bloom.
>   When your head is turned. When you look
>   away. Remove your right
>   eye. Look with your left.

You cannot cast us. Our footprints
>   are too many. You cannot tell whether
>   you peer inside windows at us or if we look out
>   of trees at you trapped in your window.

She is trying to keep us away, has been feeding us
>   potato soup and pine cones. She does not know we love her
>   potato soup. Love her stones left at the graveyard's edge.
>   We come back, follow the stone trails
>   she leaves us.

Wholecloth
(Flood)

Mother has been writing to him for two weeks since the fire and rockfall.
She says she has seen him. She says we cannot know for sure
until we lay his ghost by with four nails sunk into the corners
of his grave. She says she hears the rattle of his pick and axe
slung over his shoulder in his leather pack. She says we have
to keep writing him or he won't know he can come home. I see
Sweet Lily's shadow follow behind mother at night when she finishes writing.
She follows behind her and blows out the lamplight. The oily smoke
slides behind them. Darkness fills her scribbled page.

Mother thinks he is wrapped inside a crow that eats our corn.
Sweet Lily told us he lives down the well. Sometimes I think
he is out there in the woods with the wild children, lost
to a river or summoned by music or calling to them to gather them
home for mother, like he used to gather chickweed and teaberry.
But I know better. And I know he will return each day and empty
mother's hand of his hand. He will scratch their names into
    the lightning-struck snag.

The next morning, she will ask me for paper. I will hand her a sack.
She will not make a fire. She will not make a biscuit. She will not
remember the children that tear the air with laughter beyond the trees.
She will write him another letter, asking him to tell her stories
of witches wearing catskins and filling travelers' ears with lead,
while each of her children slip through her fingers like stitches.
We lose count of which of us are dead or living, which ones were born,
which ones return to blow out the flames as they are born each night.

New Moon

Ora knows
he is not
coming back.
She could
drown—crippled
chestnut
blue flame
or a
tide could burst—
blue heron
of lightning
lick the water,
shake the sky
like the dark
star inside a fist.

Fog

Ora watches Eli appear in the fog, knows the fog is the spiderweb in which they are dying, rising from the branches like a net. She knows he is the hand emptied of a hand, every night a eulogy.

Through the fog rags, Eli sees the abstract shadows on their porch. Wooden rail shadows like ribs of Adam. He knows the latticed light of summer, lights a candle, calls it God. He sees his cough fall out of him, crawl away on all fours.

She bends down, beckons it and it becomes a scar of stone on the frayed slope. Each step he takes sounds like tamping down earth with a trowel. Beware the river where fog rises, fills the lip of the river, the gorge and hillside caves, fills the voices of the river that say *come back, come back, come back.*

A chestnut rolls into the woods at the bottom of the mountain shaped like a crumpled skirt on the floor. Becomes an eye on a spot of sunlight through the ash. Falls asleep. Then deep in the chestnut Eli rises on fire, his clothes rinsed of coal by the flamelight.

Eli stumbles through the fog. He cannot see her. Her face is holes. Her body is an ant clinging to the neck of a bottle. It is her house. He knows that from a woman who opened the door, called to him, asked him in for supper, then left, under the kitchen floor, a blacksnake that pretends to be warm then lies on a rock in July so that it can watch Eli through the fog.

She has seen her child become an echo, find an upreaching oak tree and become a nest. And as Eli floats toward her, she sees his face moon-rinsed pale. His hand reaches forward like a lamp. He burns the fog around him like a coal, then shrinks like an ember toed by a boot.

He sees the sky missing some shingles, sees an opening to another sky. A crow pokes its head into the hole. He crouches in his feathers. Becomes the sound of cornhusks ripped from the corn. Becomes blue Kentucky ice-light. Drips up through the hole like spidersilk, early redbuds clutching the sound of her grief. No doubt it is down the well still.

O Death

One by one the cicadas clutching the brittle bark turn their spiracles to the light to breathe her in. Their breath leaves ours on the sky-veined insect wings of the world fluttering in the edge of lampglow between umbra and fire. O candle whose light we love even as your wax taper wanes. She rattles but we do not even hear her, ears pressed to the cold cookstove, to the ragged beanvines, to the dog's frothy tongue. O stone torn from the coalface, time-split and aching, receive her shaking tail of sound into each seam. Overturn each rock, unearth the pillbugs and roll their husks between fingers so she will uncoil from the corngrass and lie on a rotting barn beam where moles scurry into her open mouth, and then turn one by one their bodies inside out. O twitching cicada hull hatched one by one with her rattle. O rattle. She sheds a snakeskin rustling on our front porch step, the silent rings in which she has traveled. Our yard, filled with each year of her scaly chaff, hisses like the white undersides of leaves blowing before the flood-rains. Each day we turn our faces to the woods, to the shade curled in a fern's fiddlehead, to the shade clasped inside a hollow shell. O night, let their antennae burn.

Sunburst

A quill pokes through her pillow
        tickles her cheek. Ora remembers

            the shape of herself
        as water remembers the shape of bass swimming

through; it presses along her edges,
           over the blade of her spine.

She looks into a mirror and sees her
                bones, her eyes the road and everything
on the road. She smells her hair,
              rain-soaked woodplanks of her body,
tamps down strays, tamps the tulip bulb
             of her heart beneath earth. Lets it open:

split tuber, ache that forks through soil-silence,
        like a lightning tongue flicks through storm,
            tastes mineral. Finds it good. Returns
        to earth, like low voices, feathered, crossing water.

As though the needle of that ache struck a thimbled finger
and turned back through the cloth—
           splintered through a tulip petal, shining.

Notes

Kentucky Rose, Broken Dishes, Double Wedding Ring, Honeycomb, Jacob's Ladder, Windmill, Weathervane, Compass, Chain and Square, Log Cabin, Attic Windows, and *Sunburst* are types of quilt patterns.

Many of the poems in this book draw upon folk belief, folk literature, and other types of folklore, but especially *Ora names her children (before they are born), Gulch, Moonroot, She dreams of muddy water, Weather, Dear father, Our mother has done something strange, Laying Ghosts, Supper*, and *Burying*.

Kentucky Rose was inspired by Blue Heron and Mine 18, a former coal mining town in McCreary County, Kentucky.

Salt of the Earth borrows its refrain from the miner folk song "Down, Down, Down."

Gulch was inspired by a folk belief about owls from Harry Caudill's *Night Comes to the Cumberlands*.

Harvest Blues was inspired by "a typical working day in the life of a coal loader in the 1920s" from Raymond Densmore's *The Coal Miner of Appalachia*.

Board and Batten: Shaker screens or hoppers separated the coal into various market sizes—nut and slack, egg, and block.

Moonroot and calamus were folk medicines used to treat black lung.

Flux draws upon *Hearings Before a Subcommittee on Manufactures United States Senate, 72nd Congress. On S. Res. 178* (a resolution for an investigation of conditions in the coal fields of Harlan and Bell Counties, Kentucky), 1932.

Wild Onions uses several names from my own kin.

Dear father, Our mother has done something strange was inspired by the folk belief that to avoid miscarriage, a woman should sleep with a hatchet under her bed.

Dear Eli, I have heard we purchased a dark and bloody ground: Although since revised, an original and widely accepted translation of Kentucky's state name was "dark and bloody ground."

Flash Flood, Flash Fire: At the time, roof falls and rib rolls in mines killed and injured more underground miners than any other cause. Another cause of death were flash fires resulting from ignited finely powdered coal that collected on coal ribs and elsewhere throughout the mine.

Cloudburst is a sudden downpour common in mountain springs and rivers that causes tremendous flooding.

Black Damp is a deadly asphyxiant that reduces available oxygen content in mines.

Fractureslip is a term related to joint and fracture falls, resulting from cracks in the roof caused by fault activity. Intersecting fractures and joints can lead to roof falls.

Slickensides are smooth, glassy surfaces formed by shale, sandstone, and siltstone that can result in stackrock falls. Because of their shape, these falls were called "horsebacks" by miners.

Slake and Spall: Because of their high clay content, many shale roofs expand when exposed to moisture, which causes continuous spalling and slaking problems leading to roof falls.

Hunger and Rooting: Stackrock is a miner's term indicating stacked layers of rock. Sandstones in stackrock roofs may be weakened by mica, shale, or clay concentrations.

Kettlebottoms, another roof fall hazard, are fossilized remains of ancient tree trunks that grew in coal-region swamps and appear as tubular, conical, or bell-shaped. Trees usually grow in groups, so it is likely to encounter more than one kettlebottom.

O Death borrows its title from the Appalachian dirge.

Acknowledgments

Thanks to the editors and readers of the following journals where versions of these poems originally appeared: *Bellingham Review, Cease, Cows, Composite {Arts Magazine}, Gulf Stream, The Fourth River, Friends of Acadia Journal, Indiana Review, Journal of American Folklore, Monolith, NANO Fiction, New Haven Review, The Potomac Review, Rappahannock Review, Redheaded Stepchild, Saxifrage Press, Still: The Journal, Soundings Review, Sugared Water, Tapestry, and Yemassee Journal.*

Thanks, too, to the editors at *Porkbelly Press* and *Casey Shay Press,* where some of these poems appeared in the chapbooks *Vein of Stone* (Porkbelly Press, 2014) and *Children Born on the Wrong Side of the River* (Casey Shay Press, 2015).

Thanks to Kelly, Tim, and everyone at *Airlie Press* whose attention, care, and insight on these pages was invaluable. Thank you for giving this story a home. Thanks, too, to book designer Beth Ford for her creativity and thoughtfulness.

Gratitude to my mentors and teachers Judy Jordan, Allison Joseph, Rodney Jones, Young Smith, and Tim Evans, without whom this book would not exist. Thanks to Maurice Manning, Davis McCombs, Rebecca Gayle Howell, and Andrea Jurjević for your kind words. Thanks also to the comma of my heart, Amie Whittemore.

Thanks to the *Kentucky Arts Council, Kentucky Foundation for Women, Oregon State University's Spring Creek Project*, and *Great Smoky Mountains National Park* for their generous support and time.

Finally, thanks to my momma and dadda, Sharon and Pat McCartt, for their encouragement; to my seester, Melissa McCartt Smyth, for her art and heart; and to my Granny and Papaw, Ora and Eldred Lewis, who inspired the beginnings of these poems.

And, always, to Bryan, who has read and heard each syllable in each of these poems an infinite number of times.

ABOUT THE PUBLISHER

Airlie Press is run by writers. A nonprofit publishing collective, the press is dedicated to producing beautiful and compelling books of poetry. Its mission is to offer a shared-work publishing alternative for writers working in the Pacific Northwest. Airlie Press is supported by book sales and donations. All funds return to the press for the creation of new books of poetry.

COLOPHON

The poems are set in the timeless and beautifully legible serif Sabon Roman, created by renowned typographer Jan Tschichold in 1967. It was inspired by the work of famed Parisian publisher Claude Garamond, but named for Jacques Sabon, one of Garamond's students. The titles and folios are in the award-winning fountain pen font Marcel Script Pro from the P22 Type Foundry, painstakingly modeled on the handwriting of Marcel Heuzé's letters home to his wife and daughters from a WWII labor camp.